Seven Simple Reasons
Why He Won't Marry You

Jeffrey Barlatier

KB&G

Seven Simple Reasons

Why He Won't Marry You

Published by KINGDOM BOOK & GIFT LLP
P.O. Box 291975
Columbia, SC 29229
803-736-2472
www.kingdombookandgift.com

Unless otherwise indicated, all Scripture quotations are taken from the King James Version of the Bible. Copyright © 1994, 1997, by World Bible Publishers, Inc. Used by permission of World Bible Publishers, Inc. All rights reserved.

ISBN 978-1-4357-5798-1
Printed in the United States of America

TABLE OF CONTENTS

Contact & booking information:

You can email Jeffrey directly at:

Levitikiss2000@yahoo.com

Or

www.myspace.com/jeffreybarlatier

Acknowledgements

To Madeline, the reason and the lesson behind this book. To John, Kevin, Jason, Nicole, Des, Cola, Eric, Estee and to all of my many brothers and sister's in the Kingdom of God. I would like to thank Bishop Hezekiah Walker & Elder Neil Harris and the Love Fellowship Tabernacle for instilling in me Kingdom principles. Also special thanks to Michael Green for his excellent photography work. And how can I forget, much love goes out to everyone that said I would never become anything, you guys really keep me motivated!

We loved with a love that was more than love.

-Edgar -Allan Poe

Foreword

My motivation for writing this book was spawned from seeing the body of Christ suffer in the area of relationships. There was an overwhelming pain in my heart as I prayed and asked the Lord why there were so many unmarried couples and broken relationships in the Kingdom of God. Looking out into the pews every Sunday when we gather for worship, and every Tuesday or Wednesday when we gather for bible study, I could see the faces of women who are frustrated and disappointed because the relationships they are in have reached a plateau, but have not yet reached the peak they imagined it attaining. Many women quietly ponder why their once famed Romeo and Juliet romance has now taken a sour turn to that of the Al and Peggy Bundy sitcom. A great deal of women find themselves in relationships where the man is willing to date them, call them his girlfriend and perhaps even espouse to them the urban colloquial term "wifey", but will not marry them. Many women endure these relationships, hoping that one day he will realize what he has, only to find herself, still in a stagnant relationship 6 or 7 years later. At this point, the woman reluctantly concedes to being considered a common law wife.

By speaking and spending time with the young men that are in relationships with these same young women, I listened to them tell of the many mistakes that these women make and why they will not commit to them. When I initially heard what the men had to say regarding the subject I immediately jumped to the conclusion that the men were giving excuses but not reasons. But after much prayer, research and in-depth study of the Bible, the Holy Spirit revealed to me that what I first thought to be excuses, were in fact valid reasons why (some) men won't marry the ones they are with. There are many other reasons that can be brought to light in regards to this topic, but since this book is not exhaustive, I will only discuss the reasons that have been commonly reported.

In this book, we will take a look at the seven simple reasons that men are reluctant in marrying the ones they are with. This book will not only reveal the answers to why some men lack commitment, but also give some solutions for how you can become the one that he marries. For those women who are not currently in a relationship but are patiently waiting for the man that God has designed for them, this will help you to avoid the pitfalls that many women fall into. You've been waiting for the right man to come along, the last thing you need is to have him make you wait any longer!

The foundation of this book comes from three different principles that I am forced to integrate, in order to form this ideology of dating, courting and marriage. Along with that, there are three key questions which are pertinent to the argument in regards to those women who are seeking marriage but to no avail. The first is why won't he marry you? The second question is, is he for you? And lastly, what does God think about him? Though the question of what does God think about him, come last numerically, it is certainly not the least important.

For centuries the question of why he won't marry me, has been on the minds of many women. Unbeknownst to them, this is a question that is also on the minds of the same men that are courting these women. These men struggle with the reasons why they will not take the next step forward and commit, but would rather take a step backward and be content.

Before delving into the 7 reasons why he won't marry you, I must first lay some ground work. The foundation must be first established if we are to understand the conundrum of why he will not take the next step toward marriage. There are three principles to this foundation:

The first principle that I must present in this case for marriage is: there is no true marriage without God at the center of the relationship. I know many writers and poets declare that love must be at the center of a relationship, but what is love? Is it the butterflies in your stomach every time that person walks into the room? Is it writing that person's name over and over again because you have been thinking about them all day long? Or is love simply a feeling? If love is indeed a feeling, then that explains how you can be in love with a person one day, and not be in love with them the next. Consequently feelings come and go. Some days you're happy and some days you're sad. Some days you feel like going to work some days you don't. Sometimes you feel like talking and sometimes you don't. If love is a feeling, and feelings come and go, then your relationship is only relative. Anything relative is always changing; it is always dependent on something or someone else. It depends on the mood, the time, the weather. It just depends. On the contrary the Apostle John declares in the first chapter and the fourth verse of his 1st epistle, "Beloved, let us love one another, for love is of God; and every one that loveth is born of God, and knoweth God. He that loveth not knoweth not God; for God is love." The Apostle John defines love as God, an absolute. An absolute is that which is unchangeable, and independent. John uses God, an absolute, as the meaning of love rather than interpreting love as a relative feeling. Love is more than what you feel, it is what you know. I may not *feel* like anyone loves me, but I *know* that someone loves me. Knowing the right definition of love will allow us to look at relationships with the proper perspective.

The second principle is: before your boyfriend asks you to marry him, he should ask God if he should marry you and you should ask God if you should marry him. Traditionally whenever a man wanted to ask for a woman's hand in marriage he would first have to solicit the permission of both parents, more importantly the father. Presently, parents are grateful even to be invited to the wedding! Eloping is at an all-time high, city halls have never seen so many walk-ins, and common law marriages are commonplace. Why is our Eternal Father the last one to be asked in regards to whom we marry?

Look at the words that are used in traditional wedding vows:

"Dearly beloved, we are gathered here in the sight of

God, and in the presence of this company, to unite __

and __ in holy matrimony."

The Chaplain, Priest or Pastor begins with his introduction "we are gathered here in the sight of God" because it is God who instituted the first marriage in history, Adam and Eve. Without God marriage would not exist for it was He who created it. Trouble arises when the officiate says "Dearly beloved, we are gathered here in the sight of God" and God is surprised by the fact that you have already chosen your spouse and He is the last to know. God is in the beginning of the vows, so He must be in the beginning of your relationship. If God is introduced into your relationship at any other time, then He can only be a Savior. But if he is introduced in the beginning of the relationship then He will be Lord. The difference between being Lord and being a Savior is that, the savior is HE whom saves, but the Lord is HE whom rules. If God rules in your life then every step is ordered by the Lord and mistakes are few, if any. If he is a Savior then mistakes are plenty but he will save you from them. Always remember "Prevention is better than treatment"

The third principle that must be established is: the man must have a job. This may seem like a cliché but let me explain. This dogma originates from the book of Genesis which is the book of beginnings. Let us look at the account so we can glean from the wisdom which is hidden in the vocabulary and language that Moses used when writing this book:

"The LORD God took the man and put him in the

Garden of Eden to work it and take care of it."

Genesis 2:15

The first standard that God instructs Moses to record in the book of Genesis in regards to man, is that the man is working. Why is this important? It is important because before a man searches for a wife, he must first search for work. The reason being, before you bring anyone into a relationship with you, the provisions must be already set. Before God made Adam, HE made provisions for him. HE didn't make Adam, and then make the provisions, but rather HE made the provisions first then made Adam. Man now being created in the image of his maker, follows suit. Adam works, makes provisions then his wife steps into the scene. Eve doesn't step on the scene while Adam is in between jobs, nor does she step onto the scene while Adam is job hunting. If man is looking for a girlfriend then, its ok for him not to have a job, but if a man is looking for a wife, it is unacceptable for him not to be employed. It is while a man is working that he will ultimately find his soul mate. Too many relationships are strained because of men that choose to do the latter first.

In Genesis 1:26 Moses writes **"And God said, Let us make man in our image, after our likeness: and let them have dominion over the fish of the sea, and over the fowl of the air, and over the cattle, and over all the earth, and over every creeping thing that creepeth upon the earth."** In this passage God is creating man in his image and after his likeness. The definition for image is "a reproduction of the form of a person or object, especially a sculptured likeness; one that closely or exactly resembles another; a double."[1] If God is *working* when he creates the earth, man must do exactly what his maker does, work! Man, that is created in the image of God cannot do contrary to what his creator does for it is his maker that gives him identity. Identity defines who you are and what you do. The last person a woman should be courting is someone who isn't walking in the image of the creator, because it would mean he doesn't have an identity. A woman of God should never date, court or even think about a man that doesn't look or act like her Holy Father. There should be a resemblance.

[1] http://www.thefreedictionary.com/image

The first thing that God is doing in Genesis is working. Therefore it must be the first thing a man does when starting to move in towards the Genesis of marriage. Using the law of first mention as a backdrop, the first thing that any man must do before he looks for a wife is find a job. I cannot stress this point enough. Women, if you are dating, courting or even considering talking to a man, if he is not working, or at the very least looking for a job, then you don't even need to read The Seven Simple Reasons, you need to forget him and move on. This is pertinent because before Eve is introduced to Adam, Adam is first introduced to work. In the book of beginnings you can clearly see that introductions are important and they leave a lasting impression.

The second part of that principle Moses writes, after God instructs the man to work in verse 16 is "The LORD God said, "It is not good for the man to be alone. I will make a helper suitable for him."

It is amazing to see here that it is God that instigates the need before the man realizes his own state. God knows your needs before you do. So while Adam is doing the work of God, God sees his need. Why is that important? The bible records in the book of St. Matthew 6:33 "But seek ye first the kingdom of God, and his righteousness; and all these things shall be added unto you." This brings hope for those who have their priorities in order. God says don't worry, I will take care of the need, just seek the Kingdom of God first, and in Genesis this is exactly what Adam is doing. When you work for God, it has benefits.

Did Adam go to God saying its not good that im alone? No! In fact, the scripture says that God said that it was not good, not Adam. The word *good* here, in the Hebrew means *pleasant, agreeable, or appropriate*[2]. It does not necessarily mean that it is a negative thing or an evil thing for a man to be alone, but it's not an agreeable or a pleasant thing. Eleven times before Genesis 2:18, God proclaims everything else that he made was good. Everything God saw up until this point was good. But when God sees his son, Adam working, there's something that doesn't look pleasant to his eyes. The second part of that same verse says: *I will make a helper suitable for him.* Two points must be made here. The first is that God will make Adam a helper and the second is that everyone that is a helper must be suitable. For any man that has ever thought in his mind that there is no one out there for him, I beg you to reconsider your position on this false ideology. There is someone that God has specifically made for you, not found for you. The bible declares in the book of Proverbs: He, who *finds* a wife, *finds* what is good and receives favor from the Lord[3]. Genesis declares that God made the woman, not found her. As long as she is

---

[2] http://www.htmlbible.com/kjv

[3] Proverbs 18:22 NIV

made, she is only made with the intention that she will be found. There is a woman out there for you and you only. The word that is used here to describe the kind of person that God has specifically designed for you is *suitable.* The definition for suitable is *appropriate to a purpose or an occasion, proper, right.* One night my wife and I decided to go on a date to a new restaurant in Philadelphia. I hadn't eaten the entire day, so I was in a bit of a rush to get to the restaurant. I quickly put on my jeans, tennis shoes and a sweat shirt. I waited downstairs for my wife to get dressed. When she finally arrived she looked stunning. She asked me why I had on tennis shoes and I said "why shouldn't I have them on?" My wife said "Sweetie, didn't you look online? It's an upscale restaurant and what you're wearing is not appropriate." In other words it wasn't suitable. She told me to go and put on the outfit she had bought me for my birthday, because it was proper, just right for the occasion. The person that God has fearfully and wonderfully made, designed and sculpted for you is waiting for you. It is up to the man to find her and not the other way around. God does the making, but the man does the finding.

Complete abstinence is easier than perfect moderation.
- *Augustine, St.*

Chapter One
Reason #1
You give him Milk for Free

I know we have all heard the cliché "why buy the cow if you can get the milk for free", at least one or more times in our lives. Well it's really not a cliché, its reality. Most women are not married because they have given away the incentive to getting married, which is sex. Sex is not the overall goal of getting married but it is an incentive for doing so. Where there is no incentive there is no motivation. One example can be found just in your walk with Christ. Our overall goal is to go to Heaven. We believe in Jesus Christ, and we live according to his statutes and commandments, not because it's an option but because it's required. In living according to his statutes and commandments there are certain rewards that one gets when doing so. The bible says "No good thing will he withhold, from those who walk uprightly[4]". Living holy is required but there is an incentive for doing so. Perks, incentives, benefits, sign-on bonus; all these words have the same meaning. The incentive is the fuel for motivation to get to the specific destination. Women get tripped up when they confuse the fuel for the motivation, when the fuel is what drives the car (your relationship) to the specific destination   (marriage).Where there is no

---

[4] Psalm 84:11

incentive, motivation eventually dies. It's not that he doesn't want to get married, he just isn't motivated to do so, and the incentive that was supposed to be used to get both of you to the altar has only gotten you into the bed, and no further. Sex does not equal marriage, but marriage equals sex.

Solution: No More Milk.

Benefits:

The first benefit is that you will now be walking in the will of God, and you won't be considered a sinner (unless there is another area in your life that is not totally crucified). The second benefit is that he will pay more attention to you and you will resurrect your relationship back to where it first was when you started dating. The phone calls will increase, the flowers will keep coming and marriage will be a hot topic between the both of you. He will love you even more because he has already tasted of your heavenly goodness and will want to ensure that he is the only one that will ever have that opportunity. It will also make him a little insecure. Being insecure in this case is not necessarily a bad thing as some might presume.

Side Effects

After giving him what most men truly desire, he becomes accustomed to it. Eventually IT and YOUR value become depreciated. Tell him you will no longer engage in any, and I mean ANY intimate activity (kissing, touching, any other physical act that brings pleasure between two people). At first he will think it's a joke. In his mind he will immediately say "Yeah right, I can get it when I want, whenever I want." So you better believe he will be more aggressive and more persuasive than ever before. Not so much so that he can get a release from pent-up sexual tension, but to prove to you and him, who is really in control. In the 7th chapter of I Corinthians, the Apostle Paul declares that the body of the husband is not his but is for the wife, and the body of the wife is not hers but the husbands. Your boyfriend has exclusive rights that he has not signed a contract for, or made a covenant between you and God for. Be prepared for him to come on to you more strongly, but the bible says "submit yourselves unto God, resist the Devil and he will flee.[5] The only way you can resist your boyfriend is if you submit yourself unto God. Your "No" must be stronger than your previous "yes".

By telling him that you no longer will indulge in intimate activity before marriage, he might use this as an exit to move on to another woman. If that is the case then he was never for you anyway. If the absence of sex is an excuse to exit then he's doing you a favor. What would happen when you're married and a day or time came when you just didn't feel like having sex or were too tired to perform? Would he move on to another woman then? On the other hand, since you already let him taste of the forbidden fruit he might already have an appetite for it, and will most likely stay, but a lot of prayer and deliverance is necessary. He may possibly begin to treat you badly or try to make you feel guilty in an

---

[5] James 4:7

effort to make you succumb to the sexual habits that you've already established. He may tell you that there are a lot of other women that he could sleep with at any time in an effort to make you give in. He might try to promote all of his good qualities to make you "snap out of it, and realize what you're missing". He may try to make you believe that he is insecure in the relationship, and what better way to alleviate those feelings of insecurity than with your body? He may even tell you that you're getting married anyway so you might as well do it. All that I listed above are different forms of mental manipulation. There are more but they all have the same intent. They are to make you give up and give in. Sorry fellas. Women, stick to what's right and you will get not only what you want, but what you deserve. Try to remember this...each and every time you lay with him and give him your body, you add another 6 to 9 months of waiting to get married. If you show him this part of the book and say this is why we can't do it (have sex), he will tell you that this is a lie! Whatever it takes will be his motto. You know what's the irony of this whole situation? If he is truly a man of God, a man after God's own heart, after he finishes sleeping with you, he will feel guilty. So by saying NO, you help him and help yourself. Trust me.

Do you love me because I'm beautiful, or am I beautiful because you love me?

-Oscar Hammerstein, II

Chapter Two
Reason #2
You Let Yourself Go

I know, I know! You're ready to skip this one and jump to number 3 or even throw this book in the garbage, but this is one of the most important reasons why he won't marry you. Let me explain. A beautiful blonde was asked would she rather have beauty or brains. She replies "I would rather have beauty instead of brains because the average man can see better that he can think". What's the moral of the story? Men like to look at beautiful women. Not necessarily to lust but to admire. Do you remember the first time he was checking you out? How did it make you feel? Now let me ask you this, when was the last time he looked at you like that? The way you looked when he first met you is what made him totally infatuated with you even though he didn't know you yet. Why? Men are visual creatures. When he first saw you he didn't tell you what a beautiful brain you have, that came later, and your looks came first. Let me give you some scripture to back up my claim. The Bible declares that "Man looks at the outward appearance but God looks at the heart".[6]   A lot of attention is given to the second part of the scripture but take a look at the first part. The Bible says what men look at. I didn't make it up.   Men presume your outward appearance to be a shadow of what is stored on the

---

[6] I Samuel 16:7.

inside. This may sound shallow, but if you are looking for a man to say that he likes you for your inside instead of your outside then you are expecting the wrong thing. Think about what the man is saying when he says he likes you for your inside and not your outside. It's almost an insult and may cause you to be insecure and suffer from low self-esteem. If the Bible says that man looks at the outward lets take care of what God gave you and what man is looking at.

Beauty is a gift from God. And every woman is beautiful in the eyes of some man. If there is something about you that you know he likes the most, accent it and take care of it. If he says that he likes that you're petite then do your best to stay petite so you can stay pleasing to the eyes of your future husband. If he says that you have pretty feet, make sure they are always done and don't try to squeeze into shoes that are too small and develop corns. If he says you have pretty eyes, don't wear shades, get your eyebrows done and take out those contacts. If he says that you have a nice shape, keep it like that. If he likes your hair long don't experiment and cut it short. In doing so, you will probably impress people but not the one you're trying to marry. Spending time and money impressing people that won't contribute anything to you is time consuming and expensive. Impress your man, for it is he that will make the greatest contribution to your future. It always baffles me when a woman can spend hours getting her hair ready, picking out the right clothes, getting her eyebrows done, getting her nails done, and makeup done to go to an event to impress people that will never know her name, never put any money in her checking account or even compliment her on how stunning she looks, but when she's in the presence of the man she is courting, she doesn't even invest half the energy, time or money.

Women, your looks are IMPORTANT! Your mind is also important but that's not the topic at hand. (Don't worry we will get to that) When your boyfriend/future husband begins to see you losing your looks, it can scare him away. They start to look at other women more and pay you less attention. Men can look at a woman passing by and say "wow, she looks pretty but my girlfriend looks better, or just as good." But if he ever says "wow, she looks pretty and my girlfriend needs to go on a diet," or "she hasn't gotten her hair done in three weeks," then you're in the danger zone. I was talking to a young man a couple of weeks ago that said to me, he was thinking about really getting serious with this one young lady but he was afraid that another woman would come around that looked prettier than her and he would be trapped? Sounds shallow right? But it's the truth. And it's a simple truth. I told the young man, that as long as you walk on this earth, there will always be someone that looks better than your mate, just like there will always be someone that looks better than you! I also said that it's the same thing as having a nice car. Car manufacturers will always come out with a new model vehicle that looks better than the previous model cars. But as long as when you finish looking at that other nice car, you can get in your car and still admire what you have, you'll never regret making your decision. And there are some model cars that no matter what new car comes out, they still can't compete with the older models. (I.e.2001 Lamborghini Gallardo)

Men always want to feel they are marrying the best. That means the best in every area. You may not feel that you are America's Next Top Model, but as long as you are to him, that's all that really, matters. Beware if he hasn't given you a compliment in a few weeks. If something physical about you has changed and he complains about it, don't get upset and tell him about his gut, do something about it! Then tell him about his gut!!

Solution: Have a ME day

A ME day is when it's all about you. If you have children get a babysitter and take yourself out. Splurge a little of that hard earned money on yourself. Paying your bills is important but so is keeping your man interested in you. Go to a day spa; get your hair, nails and toes done. Get a nice relaxing message. Go shopping. Buy something nice. Price is not important today. As long as whatever you buy goes with your look, there is nothing too expensive. We invest in so many things why not invest in yourself, because consequently making your man happy will in return make you happy.

Benefits:

It will rekindle the desire that he has for you and that desire will motivate him to make sure he is the only one with all access. This will also give you an extra boost of self-esteem.

Side Effects:

This will in fact make him want you even more. But remember Reason #1! This is not to make him want to sleep with you; this is to remind him that you're the *"baddest"* thing he has ever laid his eyes on. As long as you remember reason # 1 and what your ultimate goal is (marriage) you will be fine. Just don't lose focus.

When a woman behaves like a man why doesn't she behave like a nice man?"
 - Dame Edith Evans

Chapter Three
Reason # 3
Who's the Man in the Relationship?

There are some men who like being told what to do. What to wear, wear to go, how to speak and what to eat. They do exist, they really do. But if you're reading this book, the man you are with is not this type of man. Want to know how I know? If he was this type of man, you would have made him marry you already because you would have told him too! Women you have to be extremely careful, because this is where a lot of women lose the battle. We know that you are beautiful , and that you were on the honor roll seven times and that you are the Vice President of your company and that you're the highest paid lawyer in the firm and that you have $65,000 in your savings account and your credit is impeccable and that the hair on your head is really your hair and if it isn't it's the most expensive weave money can buy (Remy) and you have a Master's and a Doctorate degree and you own your own company. We know that. But who is the man in your relationship? I believe (and this is just my opinion) that the more achievements and the higher up the corporate ladder a woman goes, the more difficult it is for the woman to be the wife and not the husband. It must be very difficult for you to come from a job where you are in charge of 300-600 employees, which are composed of both men and women, you have your Master's degree hanging on the wall in your office, and you make over six figures but the man you happen to be in love with has a GED, works at a job he hates, and on top of that only makes $35,000 a year. That has to be rough.

It must be difficult knowing that you make more than your boyfriend and although he may not say anything, deep down inside, you know it bothers him as well. You have your own house, while he rents a room. You have great credit but the bill collectors won't stop calling him at home and at work. You drive the new Mercedes Benz and he takes the train. You don't even remember when you get paid and he lives paycheck to paycheck. You wear Louie and he wears Lugs. You wear Gucci and he wears GAP. You wear Fendi and he has a felony. But you know that this is the man that God wants you to be with.

There is something about him that whenever you get around him it's like he makes all your problems go away. He always gives good advice. He's a good listener. He doesn't like asking you for money because he wants to work for his. He's a work in progress. He's under construction while you're open for viewing. How do you handle something like this? These are the times that we are living in. Women have the highest paying jobs. The churches are packed with working women that are about their business. They accepted Jesus and they're already making six figures. They are our co-workers, supervisors and vice presidents. This makes it all the more difficult for them, being a leader at work to become a follower at home. She can be the prettiest woman on the face of this earth and she can be the most anointed woman that has ever lived, but if she cannot play the part of the woman (a help meet), she will always be without a man. You know why? Real men are looking for wives, not husbands. I thank God for all the women that have accomplished all the things that they have set out to do in their lives. Those women are an inspiration to us as men. But don't forget, you can't hug a degree. Your money can't wrap big arms around you and in a baritone voice say "Baby don't worry God is going to work it out". You can't cuddle, hold or kiss your accomplishments. What is an accomplishment, if you have no one to share it with?

Solution:

Be the woman that God has made you to be. Don't be manly. Know your place in your relationship. Don't emasculate your man because you have more than him or know more than him. He already knows you know more and make more; you don't have to remind him. Even if he is in a peasant state, treat him like a king. Push him to be great. Encourage him. Motivate him. Keep telling him how great he will be one day. Stay humble at all times.

Women have powers that they are totally unaware of, and if you would just tap into it you could make your prince into a king and he wouldn't even know it was you. Women have the power to have men do practically anything they would want them to. But you have to know when and how to use that power. The best way to use it is through prayer and subtly. Brute force will get you no where.

A woman can make any Samson tell her where his strength is and not even sleep with him (read the story again). A woman can make Adam eat what God told him not to eat. A woman like Jezebel can have every prophet killed and her husband say nothing about it. A woman like

Esther can save a whole Jewish nation by her beauty and submissiveness. Women have such a powerful affect that God likens the children of Israel to a wife and as the apple of his eye. Women are so important that the church is called the Bride of Christ. Women are so important that even though Adam was in the presence of God, God said it wasn't good for man to be alone. Women are so vital that God uses them as vehicles to bring in new life.

Woman, do you realize who you are? Do you realize the power that lies within you? A little of that power peeks out at work, at school or at church but the power has not truly manifested until you use it in the life of your husband. You are more important and powerful than you think.

Benefits:

Besides being in the will of God, you will give your man a boost in his self-esteem. A woman can make a man into whatever she wants him to be. What you speak into his life can happen before your very eyes. He may be under construction, but there will be an unveiling one day.

Side Effects:

Besides all of the brothers complaining to their girlfriends and wives that they need to be more like you, there are no real negative side effects. You will become the epitome of what a girlfriend is and even his friends will repeatedly say to him "You better hurry up and marry her before someone else comes and snatches her up!" You might have to hold your tongue for a while and not say what you really want to say to him, or what deserves to be said. A few of your single friends will tell you that you're crazy but of course they are the ones that are still single, divorced or undercover lesbians.

I am a woman in process. I'm just trying like everybody else

-Oprah Winfrey

Chapter Four
Reason #4
You're a Liability and not an Asset

Another reason your man doesn't want to marry you is because he sees you as a liability instead of an asset. What I mean by that is you bring more problems to the table than you do solutions. You having 2 children from 2 different fathers, we can work with that, but your issues are another story. You're beauty is what attracted to him to you and you have a few traits that enjoys but what else do you have to offer? Is that it? The tables are now turned compared to the previous scenario in Reason #3. Your boyfriend has good credit, a good job, benefits, 401k, money in his savings account and excellent spending habits. You have bad credit, you work at a job that doesn't pay well, you go shopping every time you get paid because you feel like you work hard for your money and deserve it. You haven't paid off your student loans, you don't have a degree and your spending habits are the worst.

Some might feel as though these things are not important but any married person will tell you, two of the biggest reasons for divorce are adultery and financial trouble. "There is no romance without finance" is a very true saying. The man is coming to the table prepared and all you have to offer him is your looks? I know I told you men are visual creatures, but after we finish admiring your beauty, we want to know what you have to offer, because beauty is not enough. Take a look at this email that a woman posted on Craigslist. Then take a look at the response that followed:

What am I doing wrong?

Okay, I'm tired of beating around the bush. I'm a beautiful (spectacularly beautiful) 25 year old girl. I'm articulate and classy.
I'm not from New York. I'm looking to get married to a guy who makes at least half a million a year. I know how that sounds, but keep in mind that a million a year is middle class in New York City, so I don't think I'm overreaching at all.

Are there any guys who make 500K or more on this board? Any wives? Could you send me some tips? I dated a business man who makes average around 200 - 250. But that's where I seem to hit a roadblock. 250,000 won't get me to Central Park West   I know a woman in my yoga class who was married to an investment banker and lives in Tribeca, and she's not as pretty as I am, nor is she a great genius. So what is she doing right   How do I get to her level?

Here are my questions specifically:

- Where do you single rich men hang out? Give me specifics- bars, restaurants, gyms?

-What are you looking for in a mate? Be honest guys, you

won't hurt my feelings!

-Is there an age range I should be targeting? (I'm 25)

- Why are some of the women living lavish lifestyles on the Upper East Side so plain? I've seen really 'plain Jane' boring types who have nothing to offer married to incredibly wealthy guys. I've seen drop dead gorgeous girls in singles bars in the east village. What's the story there?

- Jobs I should look out for? Everyone knows - lawyer, investment banker, doctor. How much do those guys really make? And where do they hang out? Where do the hedge fund guys hang out?

- How you decide marriage vs. just a girlfriend? I am looking for MARRIAGE ONLY

Please hold your insults - I'm putting myself out there in an honest way. Most beautiful women are superficial; at least I'm being up front about it. I wouldn't be searching for these kind of guys if I wasn't able to match them in looks, culture, sophistication, and keeping a nice home and hearth.

THE ANSWER

I read your posting with great interest and have thought meaningfully about your dilemma. I offer the following analysis of your predicament.
Firstly, I'm not wasting your time; I qualify as a guy who fits your bill; that is I make more than $500K per year. That said here's how I see it.

7 Simple Reasons,

Why He Won't Marry You

Your offer, from the prospective of a guy like me, is plain and simply a crappy business deal. Here's why. Cutting through all the B.S., what you suggest is a simple trade: you bring your looks to the party and I bring my money. Fine, simple. But here's the rub, your looks will fade and my money will likely continue into perpetuity...in fact, it is very likely that my income increases but it is an absolute certainty that you won't be getting any more beautiful!

So, in economic terms you are a depreciating asset and I am an earning asset. Not only are you a depreciating asset, your depreciation accelerates! Let me explain, you're 25 now and will likely stay pretty hot for the next 5 years, but less so each year after. Then the fade begins in earnest. By 35 stick a fork in you!

So in Wall Street terms, we would call you a trading position, not a buy and hold...hence the rub...marriage. It doesn't make good business sense to "buy you" (which is what you're asking) so I'd rather lease. In case you think I'm being cruel, I would say the following. If my money were to go away, so would you, so when your beauty fades I need an out. It's as simple as that. So a deal that makes sense is dating, not marriage.

Separately, I was taught early in my career about efficient markets. So, I wonder why a girl as "articulate, classy and spectacularly beautiful"
as you has been unable to find your sugar daddy. I find it hard to believe that if you are as gorgeous as you say you are that the $500K hasn't found you, if not only for a tryout.

By the way, you could always find a way to make your own money and then we wouldn't need to have this difficult conversation.

With all that said, I must say you're going about it the right way.
Classic "pump and dump."
I hope this is helpful, and if you want to enter into some sort of lease, let me know.

What more can be said about this? The unknown writer said it all. You don't have to have it all, but you should have something. Something, even if it's passion, drive and a dream. I'm beginning to learn that potential is not enough anymore. When I was a little boy growing up, my teachers would tell my mother that I had the potential to be a straight A's student, all I had to do was try harder.   But I didn't want to try harder. I wanted to laugh, joke and throw spitballs. Therefore I was never a straight A student. What does that mean? Potential means nothing if there is no passion, drive and a dream behind it.   It is nothing but a car, with no steering wheel, no tires and no destination.   All I had when I met my wife was passion, drive and a dream, and look how far that has brought me. When coming into a relationship, a woman's should have more to offer a man besides her looks. In a man's eyes, looks are not what you bring to the table, looks are what gets you to the table. He has to be attracted to you even before we get to the next level.

Solution: Bring more to the table. Making a relationship work requires more than bringing 50% to the table, you have to bring 100%. If you are not in a relationship and your waiting for the man that God has for you, be prepared. The bible declares that Esther prepared for one year to meet her husband[7]. If you are not yet with the man that God has designed for you, it's a possibility that the reason he hasn't come into your life, is because you're not ready for him. Your finances are not ready, your education and your schooling is not ready. Your credit score is not ready. But you still proclaim that you have faith that the man of your dreams is on his way. You know what's the highest level of faith? Preparation! When you prepare for something , it shows God that your serious about this blessing. Women that don't prepare for husbands are always single or even worse stuck with boyfriends. There is nothing worse than being stuck with someone you know is not your husband, but because of lack of preparation, you settle for what you can afford, rather than what you desire. For those women who are in relationships and are waiting to get married, its time to step it up. Its time to go back to school, its time to clean up your credit, its time to start looking for a new job, its time to take some cooking lessons, its time to get rid of the emotional mess that was left from your previous relationships, its time to build a strong prayer life, its time to read your word daily, its time to get into ministry, its time to go to the next level!

Benefits:

You will have more to bring to the table and this should make you feel that you're contributing something to the relationship. In a situation where you're bringing nothing to the table, the other party can sometimes make you feel

---

[7] Esther 2:12

like they're doing you some great deed   by being with you. As if there adopting an orphan, or taking in someone off the streets. This is not a good feeling, and it can bring on insecurity.   If he leaves you, you have the freedom and liberty to do whatever you want, because you have yourself together. You got your money right, you're head on straight and you know which way you're going, up! Also, there will be benefits that you can enjoy and don't have to get married for. For example: Owning your own home.   Or taking vacations around the world. Not having to rely on anyone but yourself and Jesus. Having more control over your life.

Side Effects

None.

-To bring up a child in the way he should go, travel that way yourself once in a while. -Josh Billings

Chapter Five
Reason # 5
Train up a Child

This part may not be relevant to some but to those that it applies to, it's extremely important, more so than any other reason if children are involved. Having children adds a whole different dynamic to the equation. It's not just you and him, but you him and the child. There are many different variables that come into play with children. Let's start with if the child is from a previous relationship and the dad is in the picture. The dad is a genuinely good father but things between you guys just didn't work out. You set aside your differences for the sake of your child and the two of you are trying to do what's in the best interest of your child. Now, when your new man comes along, the child's father instinctively gets protective over his child and maybe, evens you, but then his reasoning abilities will kick in and remind him that you are no longer together. But the presence of another male figure and the possibility that someone may be a permanent fixture in the life of his child, without his authorization, will absolutely cause some kind of emotion to rise up in him. He's at a fork in the road, where his upbringing, spirituality, education, morals, ethics and associations will determine which road he will go down. The high road, which is the morally right and the most advantageous for all involved, is when the father accepts the fact that his child will be in the presence of another man that may potentially become his step-father. This will not deter him from continuing to be the outstanding father that he's been all along. This alone makes him an even greater father. The fact that he can set aside his pride and his ego is a virtue in and of itself.

Then we have the low road, the dishonorable and improper route that not only diminishes the bond with the child but also has the potential to create a legacy of unbalanced children. The father may be unable to cope with the fact that his child is going to be in the presence of another man who is likely to be given the title step-dad. The father might begin to minimize his presence by not showing up to important events and milestones in the child's life. All of a sudden he is never available to spend time with his child and when he does, he constitutes it as baby sitting, as if the child does not belong to him. His abundance of wealth seems to dry up and he doesn't have any money to allot to you for the child's basics needs. Taking him to court for child support is a hassle because immoral people like him usually don't have a job on the books, if he has one at all.

If allowed to, this type of father produces a child that lacks love and attention from a person they should be finding comfort and security in. The potential step-dad must now prepare to take the role of being both step-dad and at times, dad. Situations like this can be very intimidating for some men. Having to take on responsibility for a child that they didn't participate in conceiving, may seem a bit much, as if he's bitten off more than he can chew. If you have an easy-going child the prospect of being a step-dad won't seem so bad. He can begin to love the child as his own, the merger comes naturally and he'll willingly take the place of the man that walked away. But what if the picture isn't as pretty as the one I just painted? What if the child is a problem child? Unruly and disrespectful with a total disregard for authority? Then what? This kind of a child will definitely keep him from marrying you.

Solution:

If your child is the latter part of the above scenario, a problem child, and the person you're courting wants to marry you, you want to allow him to have a say so in the disciplining of your child. Too many women that have been left with the responsibility of raising a child by themselves find a potential spouse and find it difficult to let a man into their child's world for fear of future abandonment. She can handle you walking out of her life, but having another man walk out of her child's life is something she will not have. This is understandable, but there are two things I have to address in light of this:

1. Women need to be extra selective in picking of the men they allow to come into their lives. Every man should be thoroughly screened before you even introduce them to your child.

2. No man should be held accountable for another man's actions. It's just not fair.

Be careful of allowing the man that is your potential spouse free reign in the bedroom but no reign at all in the family room. What I mean by this is that you cannot allow him to give his opinion and input in the decision making process when it is in regards to things that affect the two of you but when it comes to your child, you count him out. If you're going to let him in, let him all the way in. Too many women separate the child from their relationships as if it's a side matter that only they have to deal with. This is a major fallacy. The Bible states that when you are married, the two are now one. What that means is your problems are my problems, and your issues are my issues. A beautiful example of this can be seen in the State of New Jersey's Legislative Laws. Any bill that is sent to a collection agency goes on the credit of the spouse as well. If a married man or woman buys a house, both names are placed on the deed. Why? Because the State of New Jersey has an understanding that the two are now one. That's why being selective in the dating process is imperative to your present and drastic to your future. One wrong decision can mess up your whole future.

Side Effects:

There will only be a side effect for this solution if you are not selective in the choosing of whom you date, possibly court and potentially marry. The wrong person will and can damage you and your child's life. Your child might begin to believe he is the cause of men coming in and out of his and your life and not staying. Again, I emphasize, be very selective. Selection involves thorough screening, prayer and confirmation from God.

Success in marriage does not come merely through finding the right mate, but through being the right mate.

-Barnett R. Brickner

Chapter Six
Reason # 6
He who finds a wife...

It's hard to believe that some people have not heard this scripture before. Besides the "no weapon that is formed against me shall prosper," this has to be the second most quoted scripture in the Bible. Why? Well, marriage was the first institution that God constructed on the earth and marriage is also an example of God's relationship towards his people. Throughout the bible, you can find examples of how God refers to his people as his "bride" (Jeremiah 2:2, Revelation 21:2), or even as the "apple of his eye" (Zechariah 2:8).

In Proverbs 18:22 Solomon asserts that "a man, that finds a wife finds a good thing," and on top of finding something good (as if that wasn't enough) they obtain the favor of the Lord. A problem arises when men that have an understanding of this scripture fear that the woman that they are marrying is not a wife, but simply a girlfriend. Many women have been taught or have learned through experience or visual observation how to become a good girlfriend but have lacked the fundamental principles of being a wife. Learning to be a girlfriend begins early in life but learning to be a wife begins late in life.

Training in the School of *"Girlfriendism"* begins in elementary school. It's innocent enough. You might hold hands; share your candy and sometimes a peck on the lips. As the years go by and you gain experience. The acts begin to evolve. You go on dates to the movies, go to parties, and watch T.V together, send emails, shoot each other instant messages, take late night phone calls, make sure they're number one on your myspace page, kiss, and hug. These are just some of the attributes of being someone's girlfriend. But being a girlfriend and being a wife are two totally different things. A man that is looking for marriage does not look for a girlfriend, he looks for a wife.

In looking for a wife, the mind seeks for qualities, attributes and skills that he feels that he needs to have in his wife. If this man has had a close relationship with his mother, then his selection process is all the more difficult. Why? Because he has the perfect example to compare and contrast with. He'll juxtapose every girl he has an attraction to and compare them with his mother. And if the woman does not fit the criteria or match up, he won't break up with her, but he will put into the girlfriend category. Not the wife category. Why is being put in the girlfriend category a bad thing? If a potential wife comes along, you're nothing but a girl that is a friend (girlfriend); and you can easily be cut out of the picture.

The woman that is the potential wife may not be 100% equal to the man's mother, but there can be some comparison in some areas. Genesis 2:24 declares that "For this reason a man will leave his father and mother and be united to his wife, and they will become one flesh." Notice in this text God shows how transition will occur, the man is to leave his father and mother and be united to his wife. The man is to leave his parents, those who have loved, nurtured and trained him up to be united to a woman so that they become one. This would suggest that the man leaves his parents to go to an even greater level of love, comfort and training. Anytime God tells you to leave and go somewhere else, it's only because he wants to take you to the next level. In Genesis 12:1, God instructs Abraham "leave your country, your people and your father's household and go to the land that I will show you." Abraham gets the commission to leave because God has greater for him in the next dimension that He has prepared.

If your man is apprehensive about marrying you, it may be because you are a good girlfriend but he doesn't see you as a good wife.

Solution:

Begin to show him that you do have the capabilities of being a good wife. Instead of ordering out all the time, make a nice home cooked meal. When he comes over make sure your house is clean. When he has a problem don't push him off by giving him answers like "I don't know," or "ask the Pastor," give him some feedback. Set aside some time to pray on your own (every Christian man finds a praying woman attractive). Call your own fast, or when he wants to come over and watch television whip out the good book (Bible) and read together. A woman that knows the Word is even more appealing. Build a bond with his mother. See what attributes you can glean from her. If he is going to be in your life forever you might as well learn from the person who has taken care of him most of his life. And last but certainly not least, learn not to talk so much, silence often speaks louder than words. I can attest that out of the hundreds of men that I interviewed, talking too much is one of the things men despise about the women they are with. Talking a lot, especially at the wrong time, may seem good to you but to most men its' seen as nagging.

Side Effects:

There are no side effects. Everything that you begin to implement will have an impact on him but more so will have an impact on your relationship with you and God. Doing what I suggest will make you an even greater woman than you already are.

I believe that nothing happens apart from divine determination and decree. We shall never be able to escape from the doctrine of divine predestination - the doctrine that God has foreordained certain people unto eternal life.
-Charles Spurgeon

Chapter Seven
Reason # 7
You are the Elect of God

I know you're probably wondering "why did he have to go there?" or "what is he talking about?" or worse "now he wants to get deep", but this is definitely not the case. The first 6 reasons are practical demonstrations of why he won't totally commit to you. It is safe to assume that you have at one point in your life heard one or two of these reasons before or even thought of them yourself. But what if none of them apply? I have spoken to and even counseled some couples that seem perfect for each other. They have the same interests, goals and ideas and seem to have a future going for themselves. But for some reason they both (or at least one of them) agree that the next step for them; marriage, doesn't seem like a good option. Why is that? Ever hear the saying "everything that feels good ain't good for you?" There is wisdom in that saying. Just because he SEEMS like the right choice, doesn't mean he IS the right choice.

For some people, making a wrong choice is *not* expensive for them. Marrying someone to them is like test driving a car. If you don't like it in a couple of weeks, you can take it back to the dealer and tell them you don't want it anymore. If you don't believe me just look at what goes on in Hollywood. But for those who are the Elect of God, bad decisions are very limited and too expensive. When I say limited I don't mean they don't have the capability, and when I say expensive I don't mean financially (even though sometimes it can be).

Anyone who is the called or the Elect of God can attest to the fact that they tried to do their own thing but it didn't work. For example, you and your man friend made plans for the hotel but the babysitter cancelled and now you can't go. Or you and your friends were on your way to the club but you got a flat tire. Or you made plans to go to a motel and found out all the rooms were booked. Or the one that I find the most intriguing, is when you already have the plans to do what you aren't supposed to be doing and you're called to a church function and in the midst of the service the Holy Ghost breaks loose and by the time the service is over all you can do is go home and go to sleep! It may seem amusing but the Elect, the Called of God cannot just do whatever they want to do. And if by chance they do get away with it (in man's eyes) the price they had to pay to do what they did would set them back so much so , that the next time they even THINK to do it again, they say "I'm good, been there, done that, cant afford it"

If I were to further expound on the doctrine of Election (the Elect of God), I would be forced to delve into the doctrine of Predestination. But since this is the Seven Simple Reasons Why He Won't Marry You, I'll keep it simple and scantly race through the surface of this dogma just to illustrate the logic in this last but certainly not the least of the reasons.

Those who are the Elect of God are those that God has both called and chosen before the foundations of the world for a specific purpose. Let me give you some scripture so you don't think I'm a heretic. Romans 8:29-30 tells us, "For those God foreknew He also predestined to be conformed to the likeness of His Son, that He might be the firstborn among many brothers. And those He predestined, He also called; those He called, He also justified; those He justified, He also glorified."

Ephesians 1:5 declares, "He predestined us to be adopted as His sons through Jesus Christ, in accordance with His pleasure and will, and verse 11, "In Him we were also chosen, having been predestined according to the plan of Him who works out everything in conformity with the purpose of His will." The Greek word rendered "predestinate" is found only in these six passages, Acts 4:28; Rom. 8:29, 30; 1 Cor. 2:7; Eph. 1:5, 11; and in all of them it has the same meaning. It's properly used only with reference to God's plan or purpose of salvation. It teaches that the eternal, sovereign, immutable, and unconditional decree or "determinate purpose" of God governs all events.

There are many scholars and theologians that oppose this view. Mainly because they deem it unfair, suggesting this principle usurps the doctrine of free will. But that is not what I am here to discuss. What I am here to discuss and bring to light for those women who have been wondering why he won't take the next step, is that maybe this person is not the one that will tie into the eternal purpose that God foreordained and predestined for you.

Everything is perfect, but it's just that one thing. He does not tie into your destiny and purpose and God has held up any and all movement in your relationship. Because you love him so much, even knowing that he doesn't necessarily fit per se, you hold onto hope that one day he will change so that he can fit. But if he was supposed to fit, he would have fit already. There's nothing wrong with him, he's just not for you. It's like seeing a nice dress, it looks exquisite, but once you try it on you realize it doesn't look good on you. The dress may look good on someone else, but it just doesn't look right on you. There are too many marriages that have failed in the kingdom of God because those who are elect have married those who were not predestined. They opted for those whom they selected on their own but were not elected from God. When this happens, it affects the entire kingdom of God. Too many seemingly perfect relationships have been elevated in the eyes of those that fill the pews only to see the same elevation turn into destruction. When the opportunity was afforded me to listen to some of these great women and men of God, at some point in their monologue they all utter the same words, "I know I wasn't suppose to marry him/her, God showed me all the signs and I chose to avoid them".

If your relationship is at a standstill, do some inventory? See if any of these reasons listed relate to your present dilemma. If none of the first six apply, there is a possibility you fall into the category of Reason # 7. Being an elect of God has its many privileges but it comes with great responsibility. You can't work anywhere you want, you can't go anywhere you want, and most importantly, you can't marry whoever you want.

Solution:

Praying, fasting and contacting your Pastor are necessary. There will be times when your feelings will speak so loudly to you that you will need your pastor, local prophet or prophetess to interpret what the will of God is for your relationship. This is why it is important to be associated with a local church and not simply have a television evangelist as your Pastor.

Side Effects:

You may have to be alone for some periods in your life only because God doesn't want you to be attached to any and everybody. And with being alone, sometimes loneliness begins to creep in along with it. In addition to much prayer and fasting, staying around people who are mature in the faith will keep you strong and focused. During these times of loneliness or solitude, these are when you should be doing your greatest work for the cause of Christ.

<u>Contact & Booking information:</u>

You can email Jeffrey Barlatier directly at:

<u>Levitikiss2000@yahoo.com</u>

Or

www.myspace.com/drjeffreybarlatier